P9-EEB-821

New Careers for the
21st Century:
Finding Your Role in
the Global Renewal

FREELANCE AND TECHNICAL WRITERS:

WORDS FOR SALE

New Careers for the 21st Century: Finding Your Role in the Global Renewal

COLLEGE OF ALAMEDA LIBRARY.

LENDING POLICY:
IF YOU DAMAGE OR LOSE LIBRARY MATERIALS,
YOU WILL BE CHARGED FOR REPLACEMENT.
FAILURE TO PAY AFFECTS LIBRARY PRIVILEGES,
GRADES, TRANSCRIPTS, DIPLOMAS, AND REGISTRATION
PRIVILEGES OR ANY COMBINATION THEROF.

New Careers for the
21st Century:
Finding Your Role in
the Global Renewal

FREELANCE AND
TECHNICAL WRITERS:

WORDS FOR SALE

by Camden Flath

MC
PUBLISHERS

Mason Crest Publishers

FREELANCE AND TECHNICAL WRITERS:
WORDS FOR SALE

Copyright © 2011 by Mason Crest Publishers. All rights reserved. No part of this publication may be reproduced or transmitted in any form or by any means, electronic or mechanical, including photocopying, recording, taping, or any information storage and retrieval system, without permission from the publisher.

MASON CREST PUBLISHERS INC.
370 Reed Road
Broomall, Pennsylvania 19008
(866)MCP-BOOK (toll free)
www.masoncrest.com

First Printing
9 8 7 6 5 4 3 2 1

Library of Congress Cataloging-in-Publication Data

Flath, Camden, 1987–
  Freelance and technical writers : words for sale / by Camden Flath.
      p. cm. — (New careers for the 21st century : finding your role in America's renewal)
  ISBN 978-1-4222-1814-3   ISBN 978-1-4222-1811-2 (series)
  ISBN 978-1-4222-2035-1 (ppb)   ISBN 978-1-4222-2032-0 (series ppb)
  1. Authorship—Vocational guidance—Juvenile literature. 2. Writing services—Vocational guidance—Juvenile literature. 3. Technical writing—Vocational guidance—Juvenile literature. I. Title.
  PN159.F58 2011
  808'.02023—dc22
                            2010011419

Produced by Harding House Publishing Service, Inc.
www.hardinghousepages.com
Interior design by MK Bassett-Harvey.
Cover design by Torque Advertising + Design.
Printed in USA by Bang Printing.

CONTENTS

INTRODUCTION

Be careful as you begin to plan your career.

To get yourself in the best position to begin the career of your dreams, you need to know what the "green world" will look like and what jobs will be created and what jobs will become obsolete. Just think, according to the Bureau of Labor Statistics, the following jobs are expected to severely decline by 2012:

- word processors and data-entry keyers

- stock clerks and order fillers

- secretaries

- electrical and electronic equipment assemblers

- computer operators

- telephone operators

- postal service mail sorters and processing-machine operators

- travel agents

These are just a few of the positions that will decrease or become obsolete as we move forward into the century.

You need to know what the future jobs will be. How do you find them? One way is to look where money is being invested. Many firms and corporations are now making investments in startup and research enterprises. These companies may become the "Microsoft" and "Apple" of the twenty-first century. Look at what is being researched and what technology is needed to obtain the results.

Green world, green economy, green technology—they all say the same things: the way we do business today is changing. Every industry will be shaped by the world's new focus on creating a sustainable lifestyle, one that won't deplete our natural and economic resources.

The possibilities are unlimited. Almost any area that will conserve energy and reduce the dependency on fossil fuels is open to new and exciting career paths. Many of these positions have not even been identified yet and will only come to light as the technology progresses and new discoveries are made in the way we use that technology. And the best part about this is that our government is behind us. The U.S. government wants to help you get the education and training you'll need to succeed and grow in this new and changing economy. The U.S. Department of Labor has launched a series of initiatives to support and promote green job creation. To view the report, visit: www.dol.gov/dol/green/earthday_reportA.pdf.

The time to decide on your future is now. This series, NEW CAREERS FOR THE 21ST CENTURY: FINDING YOUR ROLE IN THE GLOBAL RENEWAL, can act as the first step toward your continued education, training, and career path decisions. Take the first steps that will lead you—and the planet—to a productive and sustainable future.

Mike Puglisi
Department of Labor, District I Director (New York/New Jersey)
IAWP (International Association of Workforce Professionals)

The beginning is the most important part of the work.

—Plato

ABOUT THE QUOTE

As a young person, you are at the beginning of your career journey. That journey may take you to places you could never dream of today—but wherever you end up (and wherever you travel along the way), the information you gather now and the choices you consider will help you pick the best starting point for this lifelong voyage of discovery.

CHAPTER 1
WHAT IS FREELANCE AND
TECHNICAL WRITING?

WORDS TO KNOW

content: The subjects contained in a book or other written material.

citations: The footnotes or endnotes indicating the source of quoted material.

multimedia: Involving the combined use of various kinds of communications, such as sound and video.

bachelor's: The degree given after four years of undergraduate college.

master's: The degree given after a bachelor's, usually after an additional two years of graduate-level coursework.

A t a time when newspaper and magazine publishers are cutting their workforces in greater and greater numbers, when you can read an entire novel on a screen smaller than a postcard, it's easy to believe that traditional ways of reading are on their way out. Today, more than ever before, people have a choice when it comes to the way they want to read the articles, stories, or ideas they find interesting or entertaining.

While people may be turning to new ways of getting information, they are consuming more information than ever. Whether you're reading a blog post or your favorite electronic book on a handheld device that can store hundreds of books, keep in mind that while you may be getting information in a different way than people have in the past, it still took a number of people to produce that *content*, including writers.

Advances in technology and changes in the way we communicate must also be explained to new users through writing. People all around the world will need to know how to conduct business and communicate across borders using new technologies. The instruction manual explaining how to download an mp3 to your cell phone or the online document that helps you learn how to use a certain type of computer software are both examples of the sort of technical writing that will be in high demand as the technology we use changes.

When choosing a career, it's helpful to understand the changing needs of the job market. It's also important to find work that suits who you are, what you are interested in, and what you're good at. Choosing a career that fits with both what you want to do and what will be needed for the future is a great way to find satisfying work.

Careers in written communication are quickly becoming vitally important in the early twenty-first century. Freelance and technical writing is an industry predicted to grow faster than the average rate. By the end of 2018, jobs across all industries in the United States will grow by 11 percent, according to the U.S

Bureau of Labor Statistics. Jobs in freelance writing are on track to grow by 15 percent and technical writing jobs by around 18 percent.

WHAT IS FREELANCE WRITING?

Freelance writers are self-employed individuals who make their living by selling written content. This content may include material for books, magazines, news articles, or advertisements. Some freelance writers work on scripts for film, television, or theater. Freelance writers may be contracted by organizations or companies to work on a variety of writing projects. They may be hired to work on a short-term writing assignment or to work on a series of assignments. For instance, a freelance writer may be hired by an organization to provide an article for each issue of a monthly newsletter or to write a how-to book over the course of a month. Companies hire freelance writers because using a freelancer to produce written content is often cheaper than hiring a writer to work full- or part-time in-house. In addition, professional freelance writers are more likely to produce quality content than individuals in-office who may not be trained writers. Although many people write as part of their daily work or for recreation, a freelance writer is paid to primarily write.

WHAT DOES A FREELANCE WRITER DO?

Freelance writers must be able to produce many different types of written content in a variety of formats. Their material may be used in books, magazines, newsletters, advertisements, or on websites. Often writers are categorized as either fiction or nonfiction writers, depending on the material they write. For example, novelists, scriptwriters, and playwrights are all fiction writers, while nonfiction writers might produce content for textbooks or biographies. Songwriters, screenwriters, and writers working on content for radio and television broadcasts may also work on a freelance basis. Some writers work on advertisements and promotional materials, with the goal of their writing being the sale of a product or service. They might be involved in working with a client to define a brand or market a product. A growing number of freelance writers are also producing content for websites, such as scripts for web videos or blog posts.

Almost all writers research the topics they write about. This research might include using library and Internet resources, interviewing individuals, and personal observation. Nonfiction writers, in particular, are expected to produce well-researched content that includes proper *citations* in order to establish and maintain trust with editors and readers.

After researching a topic, writers must choose the information they want to convey, organize that material, and then use their own words to express ideas, communicate knowledge, or create stories. Editors will often help writers revise or rewrite their work, in order to most clearly explain an idea or factual information.

Today, both writers and editors use a variety of computer programs and electronic communication devices to produce written content. Writers are often expected to understand graphic design, page layout, and the software used to produce *multi-media* content. Writers producing content for the Internet—in the form of blog posts, news articles, or product reviews, for example—must understand the interactive elements of the web. Freelance writers working on material for websites must be able to produce content that combines text, images, sound, video, and interactivity.

With new technology entering the market constantly, more writers will be needed who are able to write technical instruction manuals.

JOBS IN FREELANCE WRITING

Freelance writers work in a variety of industries. Here are a few examples of the possible careers in freelance writing:

- translators
- journalists and reporters
- copy writers
- bloggers
- advertisement writers
- playwrights
- screenwriters, television or film
- freelance technical writers
- book authors

WHAT IS TECHNICAL WRITING?

Sometimes called technical communicators, technical writers specialize in putting complicated technical information into language that can be easily understood. As the name implies, technical writers work in industries based around technology, particularly industries related to information technology. These industries employ technical writers to develop or manage the development of technical content. Though information-technology-related companies employ many technical writers, as their industry often requires use of complex software and hardware that must be explained, other industries are hiring technical writers as well. As companies move toward using more technology-based methods to communicate with customers, to consumers, and among coworkers, technical writers are often brought in to develop technical materials that can explain issues with these systems. Technical writers also work in fields such as engineering, healthcare, and scientific industries. Any company or industry may need to employ technical writers if it uses equipment, software, or other materials that must be explained to many people who may not be experts.

WHAT DOES A TECHNICAL WRITER DO?

Technical writers produce operating instructions, assembly instructions, and how-to manuals, among other pieces of content explaining technical information. Technical writers may also create documentation for computer software or systems allowing a company to communicate with its customers. These materials are used by technical support staff, customers, and other people within a company, industry, or organization. Technical writers may work with a team developing a product in order to make the product as user-friendly as possible. It is expected that technical writers have an understanding of the products or projects on which they are working. In order to maintain their knowledge of a given subject, technology, or topic, technical writers may need to do research using libraries, the Internet, or by speaking with technical experts.

Technical writers work with scientists, computer and software specialists, engineers, customer support staff, and multimedia artists, among others. Often, technical writers are hired to manage how information is shared between groups working on a specific project or product. They may be employed to help customer support call-centers in improving customer assistance for a certain product or service. A technical writer may manage the development of illustrations, technical diagrams, charts, and other design-oriented content.

In their day-to-day work, technical writers frequently use computers and other electronic communications devices. Technical writers use a variety of computer software to create technical content that can be used on the Internet. More and more, technical writers use many different technologies and multi-media formats to explain technical information to the people who need to understand it. Technical writers may use page layout, graphic design, or web-design software to create documents and Web content. This content often features text, images, sound, and interactive elements.

Did You Know?
In 2008, 48,900 people worked as technical writers.

In 2008, 2 percent of all technical writers were self-employed. This means that they must look for work on a regular basis, just as is the case with other freelance writers. Technical writers may also be hired to work on a specific project or series of tasks, working by contract. Additionally, many technical writers are employed by technical consulting firms, which in turn may be contracted by other companies and organizations to help the flow of information between departments working on a single project, between companies working together on a product, or between companies and their consumers.

SELF-EMPLOYMENT

WHAT DOES IT MEAN TO BE SELF-EMPLOYED?

Rather than be hired for a full-time position by a single company or organization, a self-employed worker is hired for a specific amount of time or assignment, and can work for many companies or customers at once. Sometimes called freelancers or independent contractors, a self-employed worker is hired for a single job or short period of time by a company or organization in need of their skills. Companies who employ freelancers may not have people in their office who can do a certain task. Some freelancers may work as consultants, advising companies and organizations based on their knowledge of a specific topic or industry. Self-employed workers aren't part of companies, but instead work as individuals, selling their services to organizations who need them. Freelance writers are considered to be self-employed.

WHAT ARE THE BENEFITS OF SELF-EMPLOYMENT?

Self-employment allows people who want control over when and where they work the freedom to make those decisions for themselves. Rather than work in an office, someone who is self-employed may choose to work from home—or the local coffee shop. With the widespread use of wireless communication, almost any location is a possible workplace for a self-employed worker. Freelance and independent workers will also be able to choose *when* they get their work done, as long as it is completed on time. Self-employed workers are often able to set their own hours: if they're night owls, they can work till two in the morning, then sleep till noon the next day if they want. Or they can take a day off when they want and put in a marathon eighteen-hour day to make up for it (so long as they have enough energy and mental alertness to do a good job). Self-employed people also may work on a variety of projects in a given period of time, rather than a set routine of tasks.

WHAT CHALLENGES DOES SELF-EMPLOYMENT PRESENT?

HEALTH CARE

One challenge facing the self-employed is finding affordable health insurance. Many people who work full-time for salary get health insurance—that is, insurance covering medical expenses—through their work. Self-employed individuals must either get health insurance through their spouse's work or through expensive individual plans. Some states have organizations offering group health insurance plans for self-employed people. These plans allow freelance or independent workers to band together to get better rates on their insurance. In general, however, most self-employed workers will have a hard time finding affordable health insurance.

NETWORKING

Self-employed workers also need to be looking for new work on a near-constant basis. Freelancers must continue to produce work, meet deadlines, and keep in contact with employers and editors, all while searching for new assignments. Networking is a vitally important part of being successful while self-employed. Keeping in touch with old friends and coworkers, as well as former bosses is often a great way for self-employed workers to get their first freelance job, but making new contacts will help bring in additional assignments. Freelancers can also help each other find work by recommending other self-employed workers for jobs they are unable to take on themselves. Networking can be a lot of work, especially for someone who is already producing material under a deadline.

Freelance writers have the freedom to set their own schedules, but must also have the discipline to get the work done on time.

TAXES

The self-employed have to pay taxes that other people would have taken out of each paycheck. Most people have the company they work for withhold their taxes so that they only have to pay as an individual once a year. Freelancers must pay estimated taxes on their earnings four times each year. Self-employed workers must also pay into Social Security themselves, since employers pay half of their employees' Social Security taxes. When self-employed individuals file their tax returns, they also must use a different form than the majority of workers.

SELF-DISCIPLINE

The same thing about being self-employed that is so attractive to many people—the freedom to set their own schedule—can also be their downfall. It takes self-discipline to make yourself get up and work eight or more hours a day when there are no immediate consequences if you take the day off.

But self-employed workers do not have enough flexibility to procrastinate forever! People who try to get their work done in a rush right before the deadline will ultimately end up turning in work that is not their best—and eventually, they will inevitably miss deadlines. If you know self-discipline is an issue for you (are you the kind of person who studies at the last minute or pulls an all-nighter to get a project done that was assigned two months before?), then you might do better with in-house employment until you develop better work habits. Rushed, sloppy, last-minute work is the most common reason why customers don't rehire a freelancer.

FREELANCE WRITING CAREER: TRANSLATOR

Translators work with written content, changing it from one language into another. They must be able to write and communicate well, produce accurate translations of material, and have an understanding of editing. Translators don't just replace words in one language with words in another that have the same meaning; they must take into account the audience that will be reading their work. (For example, will they be children? Professionals? Academic people? What will their home country be? What will their level of education be?) This means translators may need to explain unfamiliar cultural references, make changes based on the intended reader's country of origin, or make slang in one language work in another.

Most translators use a computer to do their work. Translators keep in touch with editors as well as send and receive work via email. Some translators are assisted by special translation software that allows them to review several different versions of the same translation at once. Translators also use the Internet for research and online language tools, such as dictionaries, glossaries, or thesauruses.

Translators are hired in a variety of different industries to translate a number of different types of content. Some translators will work in many different subjects or for a wide range of

2010 Estimated Tax Worksheet
Keep for Your Records

1	Adjusted gross income you expect in 2010 (see instructions on page 6)	**1**
2	• If you plan to itemize deductions, enter the estimated total of your itemized deductions. • If you do not plan to itemize deductions, enter your standard deduction from page 2.	**2**
3	Subtract line 2 from line 1	**3**
4	Exemptions. Multiply $3,650 by the number of personal exemptions	**4**
5	Subtract line 4 from line 3	**5**
6	**Tax.** Figure your tax on the amount on line 5 by using the **2010 Tax Rate Schedules** on page 8. **Caution:** *If you will have qualified dividends or a net capital gain, or expect to exclude or deduct foreign earned income or housing, see chapter 2 of Pub. 505 to figure the tax*	**6**
7	Alternative minimum tax from **Form 6251** or the Alternative Minimum Tax Worksheet in the Form 1040A instructions	**7**
8	Add lines 6 and 7. Add to this amount any other taxes you expect to include in the total on Form 1040, line 44, or Form 1040A, line 28	**8**
9	Credits (see instructions on page 6). **Do not** include any income tax withholding on this line	**9**
10	Subtract line 9 from line 8. If zero or less, enter -0-	**10**
11	Self-employment tax (see instructions on page 6). Estimate of 2010 net earnings from self-employment $ ....; if **$106,800 or less,** multiply the amount by 15.3%; if **more than $106,800,** multiply the amount by 2.9%, add $13,243.20 to the result, and enter the total. **Caution:** *If you also have wages subject to social security tax or the 6.2% portion of tier 1 Railroad Retirement tax, see chapter 2 of Pub. 505 to figure the amount to enter*	**11**
12	Other taxes (see instructions on page 6)	**12**
13a	Add lines 10 through 12	**13a**
b	Earned income credit, additional child tax credit, making work pay credit, refundable education credit, and refundable credits from **Forms 4136, 5405, 8801,** and **8885**	**13b**
c	**Total 2010 estimated tax.** Subtract line 13b from line 13a. If zero or less, enter -0- . . . . ▶	**13c**

14a	Multiply line 13c by 90% (66⅔ % for farmers and fishermen) . . .	**14a**		
b	Enter the tax shown on your 2009 tax return (see instructions on page 6). Enter 110% of that amount if you are not a farmer or fisherman and the adjusted gross income shown on that return is more than $150,000 or, if married filing separately for 2010, more than $75,000 . . .	**14b**		
c	**Required annual payment to avoid a penalty.** Enter the **smaller** of line 14a or 14b . . . ▶			**14c**

c *Caution: Generally, if you do not prepay (through income tax withholding and estimated tax payments) at least the amount on line 14c, you may owe a penalty for not paying enough estimated tax. To avoid a penalty, make sure your estimate on line 13c is as accurate as possible. Even if you pay the required annual payment, you may still owe tax when you file your return. If you prefer, you can pay the amount shown on line 13c. For details, see chapter 2 of Pub. 505.*

15	Income tax withheld and estimated to be withheld during 2010 (including income tax withholding on pensions, annuities, certain deferred income, etc.)	**15**

16a	Subtract line 15 from line 14c	**16a**	
	Is the result zero or less?		
	☐ **Yes.** Stop here. You are not required to make estimated tax payments.		
	☐ **No.** Go to line 16b.		
b	Subtract line 15 from line 13c	**16b**	
	Is the result less than $1,000?		
	☐ **Yes.** Stop here. You are not required to make estimated tax payments.		
	☐ **No.** Go to line 17 to figure your required payment.		

17	If the first payment you are required to make is due April 15, 2010, enter ¼ of line 16a (minus any 2009 overpayment that you are applying to this installment) here, and on your estimated tax payment voucher(s) if you are paying by check or money order. (**Note:** *Household employers, see instructions on page 6.*)	**17**

Since no taxes are taken from a freelance writer's pay, he needs to make estimated tax payments four times a year. This form is a worksheet to help determine the amount of estimated taxes that are owed. The entire form can be found at: www.irs.gov/pub/irs-pdf/f1040es.pdf.

businesses and organizations, others work in a single field, becoming experts on one type of translation. Some of the most common forms of specialized translation are legal, medical, and literary translation.

Translators are also often needed to entirely localize content for a certain region or country. Localization means that content is changed not only from one language into another, but translated on a cultural level, as well. Translators who are localizing material must make it feel as though it was written in the language of the reader, even when it was created in a different place using a different language.

Many translators work by themselves and under deadline. Just like other freelance writers, translators are able to work from many different places, especially by using wireless communications to communicate with their customers. Their schedule may change each week, or even each day. Translators, as is the case with other freelance workers, must always be looking for new work. They must be reaching out to contacts and prospective employers as much as they can while completing their work on time.

Translators come to the industry with a variety of educational backgrounds. All translators must be fluent in at least two languages. Many translators grew up in bilingual households, speaking two languages since they began to talk. To prepare for a career as a translator, high school students can take courses focusing on building English, foreign language, and computer skills. Young adults looking to become translators can also benefit

What Kind of Person Are You?

Career-counseling experts know that certain kinds of people do best in certain kinds of jobs. John L. Holland developed the following list of personality types and the kinds of jobs that are the best match for each type. See which one (or two) are most like you. The more you understand yourself, the better you'll be able to make a good career plan for yourself.

- **Realistic personality:** This kind of person likes to do practical, hands-on work. He or she will most enjoy working with materials that can be touched and manipulated, such as wood, steel, tools, and machinery. This personality type enjoys jobs that require working outdoors, but he or she does NOT enjoy jobs that require a lot of paperwork or close teamwork with others.

- **Investigative personality:** This personality type likes to work with ideas. He or she will enjoy jobs that require lots of thinking and researching. Jobs that require mental problem solving will be a good fit for this personality.

- **Artistic personality:** This type of person enjoys working with forms, designs, and patterns. She or he likes jobs that require self-expression—and that don't require following a definite set of rules.

- **Social personality:** Jobs that require lots of teamwork with others, as well as teaching others, are a good match for this personality type. These jobs often involve helping others in some way.

- **Enterprising personality:** This person will enjoy planning and starting new projects, even if that involves a degree of risk-taking. He or she is good at making decisions and leading others.

- **Conventional personality:** An individual with this type of personality likes to follow a clear set of procedures or routines. He or she doesn't want to be the boss but prefers to work under someone else's leadership. Jobs that require working with details and facts (more than ideas) are a good fit for this personality.

from traveling overseas, spending time immersed in a variety of cultures, and reading in English and at least one other language. Many translation jobs will require that applicants have a *bachelor's* degree, but majoring in a foreign language isn't required. Those looking to do a specific type of translation may need to study a certain field. Employers looking to hire workers to do financial translation, for instance, may require that translators have a *master's* degree in finance. Most people who want to work as translators will need to take courses or attend conferences in translation specifically, in order to first learn how to do their work. Some fields of translation, such as medical translation, require special training.

Over the next decade, jobs for interpreters (who translate spoken language) and translators as a group are predicted to increase by around 22 percent. The increase in jobs in this field is due to increasing ties between countries around the world and the increasing number of non-English speakers in the United States. The demand for people who can communicate well in two languages is projected to grow rapidly between now and 2018.

> *Follow that will and that way which experience confirms to be your own.*
>
> —Carl Jung

ABOUT THE QUOTE

Only you can pick the right career path for you to take. Family, teachers, friends, and others may have good advice to offer you, but in the end, you must decide which is the right way for you to go. What are you good at? What do you enjoy doing most? What makes you happiest? These are good questions to ask yourself as you seek to discover your own career path.

CHAPTER **2**
EDUCATION AND TRAINING

WORDS TO KNOW

copy: The words to be printed or spoken.

nonprofit organizations: An organization that does not distribute the money it makes to owners or shareholders, but instead uses them to help pursue its goals. Charities, religious groups, and public arts organizations are often included in this category.

management-level: Having to do with jobs that will involve decision-making activities and supervising other employees. These jobs usually pay more.

liberal arts: Studies intended to provide general knowledge and intellectual skills (rather than specific occupational or professional skills).

Freelance and technical writers typically begin preparing for their career by getting a college degree, perhaps in English, communications, or journalism. High school students who know they want to become writers before they reach college, however, can do several things to prepare for a career in writing. Taking English and composition courses, for example, can help high school students become better writers and better at communicating ideas through language. Young writers can also work to get their writing published in their high school's newspaper or online. High school students who learn to express ideas clearly, communicate information well, and produce quality work under the pressure of a due date are on their way to understanding what it's like to be a freelance or technical writer. After high school, young writers should work toward a college degree, while getting as much writing experience as possible.

FREELANCE WRITERS

EDUCATION AND TRAINING

Most companies looking to hire a freelance writer will require a bachelor's degree or higher. Employers prefer degrees in English, communications, or journalism, but they may hire writers with other qualifications based on the quality of their work. Some writers may need expertise or experience in a particular field before being hired to write on that topic. A freelancer hired to write a textbook, for instance, will need to have extensive understanding of the book's subject, whether through formal education or previous work experience. Likewise, a freelancer hired to write film reviews would be expected to have a knowledge of cinema, acting, or the movie industry, in addition to the ability to write well.

Some writers may gain writing experience or fame on the Internet, writing for a blog or other website. A reputation in an online community can give a freelance writer new opportunities based on the quality of her written work, her unique way of looking at things, or the number of people reading her writing. The Internet allows some writers to gain work experience without needing a formal degree in English or communications. As always, however, employers looking to hire freelance writers will want to see quality writing as evidence of a writer's ability.

Writers can begin gaining experience while working for high school, college, or local newspapers. They may work for radio or television stations writing *copy*, or they may submit their fiction to a literary magazine. Young writers may have their work performed in high school or college theater or music departments. In addition, many young writers looking for work experience begin their careers as interns for magazines, newspapers, publishers, or broadcast stations. An internship allows a writer to learn about an industry, research writing projects, and get a chance to have his writing published, posted online, or used for broadcast.

OTHER QUALIFICATIONS

Freelance writers must be able to express themselves clearly through writing. Their writing must be logical, interesting, and easily understood. They need to be creative, curious, enthusiastic, knowledgeable about a wide range of topics, and committed to their work. Writers must be able to judge the value of researched material and be able to organize that material in a sensible way. They also must be able to work under pressure and stay on task. Freelance writers will often work under deadlines, and must be able to see a project through to its timely completion.

Understanding of communication technology is becoming increasingly important to businesses or organizations seeking to employ freelance writers. Experience with web design, graphic design, electronic publishing, and other types of media production, are all beneficial to writers looking for work as freelancers. Writers must be able to edit their own writing, use computers (or other electronic communication devices) to send their work to editors and communicate with current or potential employers. Freelance writers looking to write for online publications or websites will find valuable experience in computer software and various types of media production, as well.

ADVANCEMENT

Freelance writers will advance their careers in several ways. Working regularly and reliably with the same companies and organizations allows a freelance writer to build a reputation that can lead to future work and bigger projects. A dependable freelance writer may get work based on recommendations from past employers. Freelance writers also benefit from working on more complicated writing jobs, having their work published in more accomplished publications, or working for more well-known organizations.

Writers just starting their careers may be hired to work in a freelance capacity for small companies, newspapers, *nonprofit organizations*, or other smaller employers. Often, these jobs allow writers to be published early in their careers, gaining them experience and recognition. Advancement for freelance writers working for small organizations may be limited, however, due to the fact that these organizations will likely only have a small number of assignments for freelance writers or they may forgo hiring experienced writers who'll be more expensive to employ. Larger businesses and organizations may have more opportunities for career advancement for writers. These employers will most likely have more steady work for freelancers, more money to spend on writers, and the desire for higher quality writing.

Some freelance writers may choose to become editors working for salary. Editorial jobs are often *management-level* positions.

Finish high school. *Nearly every job requires basic communication and math skills.* Compared to workers at higher education levels, high school dropouts have more difficulty getting and keeping jobs. They also have lower earnings throughout their lives.

Plan your career. *Seek out information about occupations with favorable career prospects, high earnings, and other attributes that are important to you.* Having a solid career plan can affect your future prospects more than how much education you have. True, college study increases opportunities for careers with above-average earnings—but not in all fields. Good opportunities await workers without college degrees who spend several years learning a sought-after skill or craft.

Learn how to conduct a good job search and develop a résumé. *No matter what you do after high school, you will have to market your skills as you search for a job.* Learning about résumé preparation and job search techniques will help you get through the process more easily. Workers average more than 8 different jobs by age 32, so prepare to change jobs— even careers—until you find the one that's right for you.

Consider continuing your education. *The more education you get, the higher your earnings are likely to be.* On average, high school graduates earn more than high school dropouts. Those who receive postsecondary training earn more than high school dropouts and graduates. And workers who have bachelor's or higher degrees usually earn more than those with less education.

Develop basic computer skills. *Take advantage of every opportunity to acquire computer proficiency.* Regardless of whether you continue your education beyond high school, chances are that you will need at least minimal computer skills to do your job.

Gain experience early. *Learning by doing is a great way to approach a prospective career.* Internships, part-time jobs, and volunteer work are some examples of ways to get hands-on experience while still in school. Not only do these opportunities help you make smarter career decisions, they may help you get hired after graduation; most employers value work-related experience.

Research career information. *A small investment of your time will help you make an informed career choice that could pay dividends throughout your life.* There are hundreds of occupations, so choosing and planning a career is a lot more complex than it may appear. The ideal career for you might be something you've never heard of or thought about. The *Occupational Outlook Handbook* and other career publications are loaded with helpful information.

Value your personal interests and abilities. *You shouldn't be dissuaded from a career that interests you just because it's competitive.* If your interests and abilities draw you to a field like acting, journalism, law, piloting, or some other competitive occupation—go for it. Just be prepared for the challenges that may lie ahead.

Keep learning. *Take every opportunity to learn new skills.* The more you upgrade your skills to the constantly changing world of work, the more likely you—and your career—will adapt along with it.

This is a list of career tips for high school students by Jon Sargent at the Bureau of Labor Statistics.

Career advancement for editors often comes through promotions within a company or organization, rather than securing new and better writing jobs. Advancement may also come from moving to more reputable publications or organizations. Some editors work as freelancers, but these jobs are mostly low-level copy editing projects.

Technical Writers

Education and Training

Employers looking to fill technical writing positions require that applicants have a college degree, but they also look for knowledge in specific technical subjects and an understanding of web, graphic, or page design. Understanding of the computer software used in the production of technical materials is also important to being competitive in the technical writing job market. Employers prefer that candidates for technical writing positions have bachelor's degrees in journalism, English, or communications. Technical writers may be hired for their knowledge of engineering, medicine, chemistry, or other scientific subjects.

Certain technical writing jobs will require previous experience and a bachelor's degree or technical expertise, while others may only require a *liberal arts* degree. Technical writers applying for jobs may benefit from knowing a second language in some cases. Due to the fact that an increasing number of technical writers must be able to produce content for websites, online documents, or other web-based platforms, experience in these areas can be important to many employers looking to hire a technical writer.

OTHER QUALIFICATIONS

First and foremost, technical writers must be able to produce quality writing, express ideas clearly, and communicate well. Though their ability to communicate a message will be of primary importance to their work, technical writers must also be able to convey that message in a number of different formats.

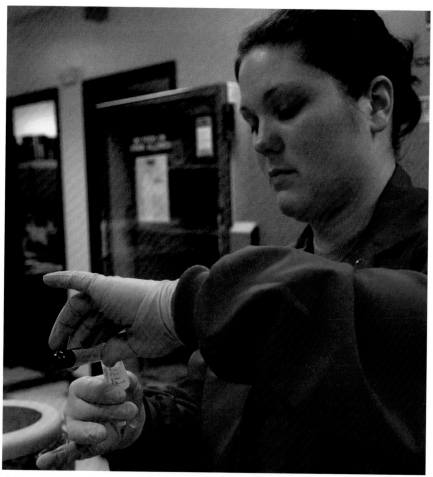

Many technical writers only have degrees in English or journalism. However, knowledge of a science, or a degree in a field like chemistry or medicine will increase the writer's chances of getting hired.

Technical writers who understand sound and video production, graphic design, and electronic publishing will have an edge when it comes to competing for many technical writing positions. Today, technical writers use a variety of computer programs that blend text, images, audio, video, and web design; experience with and understanding of these programs is also very important to employers searching for technical writers. Many employers prefer technical writers who have extensive computer experience.

Technical writers must be able explain complicated information to people who are not specialists or experts, meaning that technical writers must be good communicators who understand the way others learn and are motivated to solve communication problems, should they arise.

ADVANCEMENT

Many technical writers begin their careers in technical fields, as specialists or research assistants. They may become technical writers by developing or applying technical communication skills on the job or independently. Their experience with technical information and knowledge of a specific technical topic often helps these technical writers stand out from their peers.

In smaller technical consulting companies, technical writers may begin their careers by working on technical communication projects when they are hired. Larger companies

Did You Know?
74 percent of technical writers have college degrees.

may require that a new technical writer observe other, more experienced technical writers before taking on projects of his own. In addition, these companies may ask that new technical writers speak with specialists or experts in a specific field, in order for new employees to understand the topic (or topics) about which they will be writing. Technical writers can advance in technical consulting firms by working on more complicated or technically advanced projects, training lower-level staff, or leading a group of other technical writers. Some technical writers employed by technical consulting firms may also look for work as freelancers, in order to make more money or begin moving toward self-employment.

Freelance technical writers who provide writing on a job-by-job basis must build and maintain connections with companies or organizations that need their services in order to advance. By meeting deadlines reliably and dealing with employers professionally, freelance technical writers can establish a reputation that may help them get future work. A freelance technical writer may be able to secure long-term contracts or recurring work from companies and organizations with which she has a good relationship.

FREELANCE WRITING CAREER:
JOURNALIST/REPORTER

Reporters write news articles for newspapers, online publications, or magazines. Sometimes called journalists, reporters first research their news stories by examining documents, observing events, and interviewing people. Reporters then organize these materials and write news stories based on their research, trying to convey information about something that happened or tell an interesting story about an individual.

More and more, reporters are also asked to produce content for websites, perhaps in written, video, or audio form.

Many reporters work as freelancers and are paid by the assignment. Freelance reporters are often less costly than full-time reporters. Freelancers can offer newspapers, magazines, and online publications quality writing for less investment. Some freelance reporters may specialize in a certain field, but many will write on a variety of topics. They may be asked to produce content that can be paired with their written work and used online. Around 19 percent of writers working for news outlets worked as freelancers in 2008.

Reporters must work under deadlines, often in hectic environments. Salaried or full-time reporters may work in an office or in a large room filled with other reporters, conducting research out-of-office as needed. Freelance reporters will be able to work in almost any environment, choosing when and where to get their work done, as long as it is handed in on time.

Unlike many other careers in writing, employment for reporters is predicted to decline over the next several years. Competition will increase for fewer positions. As more full-time journalists are laid off due to budget cuts at publishers and news outlets, however, many of these companies will turn to employing freelancers. Smaller publications will provide opportunities for those looking to enter the field of journalism, as larger publications have trouble keeping their staffs. Generally, a background that includes a degree in journalism is required for young reporters looking for work.

If You Have a Realistic Personality . . .

Writing may not be the best career choice for you. Writing does not allow you to physically handle your work product the way some other career choices will. It is detail-oriented, and most writers spend most of their time sitting inside at a desk.

If You Have an Investigative Personality . . .

Here are some of the best jobs for you as a writer. (These tables also include the average salary you can expect to earn in U.S. dollars in these jobs and how many openings are projected to exist in the United States each year for these jobs. When you look at the average salary, remember that some positions will pay more than that and some less. The information comes from the U.S. Bureau of Labor Statistics.)

JOB	ANNUAL EARNINGS	ANNUAL OPENINGS
news reporters & correspondents	$44,030	50,690
broadcast news analyst	$70,730	6,310
nonfiction author	$64,560	2,140

How can I be useful, of what service can I be? There is something inside me, what can it be?

—Vincent Van Gogh

ABOUT THE QUOTE

The written word, in whatever form it appears, is a powerful tool. If you decide to pursue a career in writing, hundreds, if not thousands, of people will read your words. Your work will inspire and educate, inform and entertain. Through your writing, you will be of service to people you may never know.

CHAPTER 3
JOB OPPORTUNITIES IN FREELANCE OR TECHNICAL WRITING

WORDS TO KNOW

donors: People or companies who give money to charities.
competitive: Having to do with a situation where many good applicants are trying to get the same job.
portfolio: A collection of materials that represent a person's work.

New ways of communicating written information will give many writers new job opportunities, working for businesses who want to use the Internet to get their message to customers, newspapers who want to reach online readers, or nonprofit organizations sending e-newsletters to potential *donors*. Advances in technology also allow many writers to work in different environments, while keeping in touch with others using electronic communication. Freelance and technical writers will be able to work for a great number of different industries, writing on a variety of subjects for a wide range of audiences.

FREELANCE WRITERS

WORK ENVIRONMENT

Changes in the way we use technology to communicate have given freelance writers a wide range of options when choosing their work environment. Freelance writers may decide to work at home, in an office, or while traveling. Wireless communication devices allow writers to stay in touch by e-mail with their customers, research contacts, and editors. In addition, these devices make it possible for freelance writers to research information online, edit their work from almost anywhere, and send their writing to editors electronically. Some freelance writers may still choose to work in an office setting. Many will also conduct research that requires them to travel.

Just as freelance writers have choices in where they work, so too are they given the freedom to choose when they work. Some freelance writers may decide to work a standard eight-hour day in order to stay in touch with editors and sources, or simply because they wish to work a steady schedule. A majority of freelance writers, however, will choose their own writing routine. Freelance writers are paid

Did You Know?
In 2008, 151,700 people worked as nontechnical writers and authors in the United States.

per assignment, rather than hourly or by salary, meaning that they must be willing to work however many hours are needed to complete a piece of writing by a deadline. This includes working

Working as a freelance writer gives you the freedom to work from a home office, while traveling, or from another location.

nights, weekends, or on holidays in order to finish an assignment on time.

Though many freelance writers appreciate being able to set their own hours and work from home, the difficulties of being self-employed, including having to work on many projects at once and find new work continually, can wear on freelancers. Many freelance writers will have to work long hours in order to complete writing assignments and cope with performing under deadlines. These daily stresses can begin to take a toll on freelance writers, causing stress, fatigue, and dissatisfaction with the job. In some cases, working long hours at a computer may cause freelance writers to experience eyestrain or back pain.

JOB OPENINGS

Freelance writers may work for any number of industries, including advertising, public relations, or publishing. Some freelancers may write for television or film, though these jobs are highly *competitive* and difficult to secure. Freelance writers are also employed by nonprofits or other organizations, who may not have the resources to hire full-time or salaried writers.

Freelance writing jobs tend to be located in larger cities with thriving entertainment and media markets. In the United States, these cities include Boston, Chicago, Los Angeles, New York, and Washington, D.C. The Internet and other advancements in communications technology, however, allow freelance writers to work from any number of locations. Some freelance writers may live outside these major cities, choosing instead to travel often and keep in contact with employers and editors via the Web. For the most part, a freelance writer's location is less and less a factor in her being hired.

Did You Know?
In 2008, 70 percent of the working writers in the United States were self-employed.

EARNINGS

It's difficult to know how much the average freelance writer makes because of the ever-changing nature of freelance work. The average yearly wage for salaried writers was around $53,000 in 2008. The highest paid salaried writers earned an average of over $100,000 annually. The lowest paid among working salaried writers earned less than $28,000. In general, industries such as advertising and public relations pay writers higher salaries than the publishing industry does.

Highest Level of Education

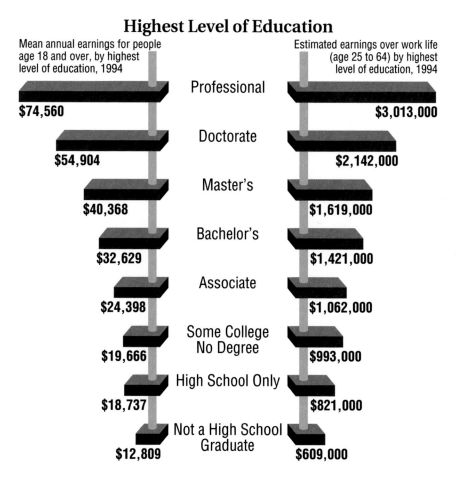

Mean annual earnings for people age 18 and over, by highest level of education, 1994

Estimated earnings over work life (age 25 to 64) by highest level of education, 1994

Level	Mean annual earnings	Estimated earnings over work life
Professional	$74,560	$3,013,000
Doctorate	$54,904	$2,142,000
Master's	$40,368	$1,619,000
Bachelor's	$32,629	$1,421,000
Associate	$24,398	$1,062,000
Some College No Degree	$19,666	$993,000
High School Only	$18,737	$821,000
Not a High School Graduate	$12,809	$609,000

Your earnings as a freelance writer will depend on a variety of factors. Education is one factor that can change your potential earnings. These numbers are old and may no longer be accurate, but they give a sense of the increase in pay that occurs with each level of education.

REAL-LIFE WRITER: NICOLE FRASER, GREETING CARD WRITER

After graduating with a four-year college with a degree in English, Nicole Fraser began writing greeting cards in her free time. She would call up greeting card publishers whenever she had time, ask if they needed any specific type of cards, and then send them drafts of her ideas for those cards. Many freelance writers like Nicole work for greeting card publishers.

Nicole's job involves watching the trends of the moment. She reads the most popular books and magazines in order to know what people are talking about. And how they're talking about it. Card writers need to know just what people are saying in conversation. "We have to know the language people are using today," she says.

Freelancer writers sell their work to greeting card publishers for anywhere between $60 and $150 per card. Nicole landed her

Freelance writers who earn income by the assignment have variable pay. Writers may be paid for articles, books, scripts, or other writing projects, with the amount they are paid changing from job to job. Due to the difficulties of finding new assignments and the frequent lack of a steady income, many freelance writers will choose to take on a second job. Freelance writers may choose this based on the benefits employment provides (such as salaried writing job at greeting card publisher American Greetings by sending them a *portfolio* of her freelance work.

Nicole says that any college major can work as a freelance greeting card writer. She recommends attending creative-writing seminars or classes, but says that an English major isn't required for a career in greeting card writing. Though Nicole started writing cards as a freelancer and worked her way to a salaried position that way, other greeting card writers start as interns or proofreaders at greeting card publishers.

Greeting card writers must express with writing what others wish they had the words to say. They may work on funny material one day and then move on to writing something tender and heartfelt the next, but ultimately a card writer's job is to get a message from one person to another.

health insurance and pension plan), since self-employed individuals must pay for these benefits themselves.

TECHNICAL WRITERS

WORK ENVIRONMENT

Many technical writers are able to choose their own work environment as a result of advances in communication technology.

Just as freelance writers are able to work from home, an office, or while traveling, technical writers can also work from almost anywhere, using computers to complete research, write and edit assignments, send work to editors, and stay in touch with their customers.

Technical writers work with professionals in technical fields from all over the world, making key skills the capacity to understand complicated information and the ability to work with people of various backgrounds.

Most technical writers are employed by organizations that use the technical material they produce to educate workers or improve communication between different groups within their organization. Technical writers may also work for technical con-

As a technical writer you will have job opportunities in a wide range of industries.

Employment of Technical Writers by Industry, 2002	
Industry	Percent Employed
Professional, Scientific, and Technical Services	31.3
Manufacturing	17.9
Publishing Industries (except Internet)	11.3
Administrative and Support Services	6.4
Government	3.9
Finance and Insurance	2.6
Performing Arts, Spectator Sports, and Related Industries	2.5
Management of Companies and Enterprises	2.3
Wholesale Trade	2.1
Retail Trade	1.7
Self-Employed	6.2
Others	11.8

sulting firms, which may hire their services out to companies or organizations looking for technical communication services. Finally, some technical writers are self-employed, meaning that they will have to cope with the same pressures that other freelance writers face. These include difficulties in having to work on multiple projects at once, continually searching for new writing assignments, and working long, sometimes unpredictable hours while meeting deadlines. Technical writers may need to work nights or weekends in order to complete writing assignments on time. In some cases, technical writers may need to be in contact with people in other time zones, requiring late nights or early mornings.

EMPLOYMENT

Though technical writers are employed in almost every industry, most technical writers work in industries related to computers, computer software, publishing, engineering, and science. In 2008, the computer systems design industry employed 18 percent of all technical writers, the most of any field. The second largest-employer of technical writers in 2008 was the computer and electronic manufacturing industry, which employed 8 percent of working technical writers. Other industries that employ technical writers include computer software publishers, architectural and engineering services, technical consulting firms, management and scientific consulting companies, and scientific research services industries. Of all technical writers working in 2008, 2 percent were self-employed.

Technical writing jobs are mostly concentrated in cities with a high number of information technology companies. In the United States, these cities include San Diego, San Francisco, Boston, and Washington, D.C. The location of work is less important than it once was, however, as more and more technical writers are able to use the Internet and other communication technology to keep in contact with clients, employers, and editors.

EARNINGS

In 2008, salaried technical writers made an average of around $61,000 annually. The highest paid 10 percent of all technical writers made an average of more than $97,400 each year. The lowest paid 10 percent made an average of less than $36,500 yearly. The majority of technical writers earned an average yearly income of between $47,000 and just under $79,000.

Median annual wages in the industries employing the largest number of technical writers were:

Software publishers	$71,640
Computer systems design and related services	64,380
Management, scientific, and technical consulting services	62,920
Employment services	61,810
Architectural, engineering, and related services	60,140

(from www.bls.gov/oco/ocos319.htm)

If You Have a Social Personality . . .

A good job for you as a writer might be a newspaper reporter, where you could spend much of your time interviewing people to get your stories. The average annual earnings for a reporter at a small community newspaper are about $27,000, but by getting experience, you may be able to move to a larger news organization, where the pay will be much greater. The average salary for news reporters across the industry is $44,030, and there are about 50,690 jobs to be filled each year.

If You Have an Artistic Personality . . .

Here are some of the best jobs for you as a writer.

JOB	ANNUAL EARNINGS	ANNUAL OPENINGS
movie scriptwriter	$98,820	2,340
freelance fiction writer	$100,600	2,140

Work without joy is a chore or a bore.

—Laurence G. Boldt

ABOUT THE QUOTE

As you choose a career, of course you have to consider practical questions: How much money will I be paid? What are my chances of being hired? What will my opportunities be to grow in this career? But keep in mind that money is not everything. No matter how much money you make, if you don't enjoy the work you do each day, your life will be unsatisfying. The secret to finding happiness in the work world is to match up your values, your talents, and your pleasures with work that the human community needs in one way or another. When you do that, the money usually follows!

CHAPTER 4
THE FUTURE OF FREELANCE AND TECHNICAL WRITING

WORDS TO KNOW
platforms: Underlying computer systems or other technology that forms the foundation on which other programs are run.

The next decade is predicted to be a good time to look for work in a variety of writing occupations. The numbers of freelance and technical writers who are employed are projected to grow faster than the average for all industries. The Internet and expanding types of electronic communications present many opportunities for writers, both freelance and technical, who understand how to use these technological advances to their benefit. Writers who can use new methods of reaching audiences will find that they have more opportunities for work and advancement than those who do not. Younger writers who have used these technologies for most of their lives will be able to take advantage of their knowledge when competing with older workers who may not be as familiar with communicating electronically.

FREELANCE WRITERS: JOB OUTLOOK

The number of jobs for writers (both salaried and freelance) is expected to grow by 15 percent, much faster than the average for all industries. Though the overall employment of writers will grow, there will be more competition for available work as more people move into the industry. Freelance writers will face a job market in which there are more writers than assignments, but due to the increase in employment, more writers will be able to find work as well.

EMPLOYMENT CHANGE

In order to meet the demands of customers in the twenty-first century, companies in almost every industry are turning to multimedia technology and web-based communication. They may have their own website, send out a monthly e-newsletter, or use a text-messaging service to stay in touch with their customers. Many of these businesses will need skilled freelance writers in order to get their messages across to consumers and clients. As the number of quality online publications grows, many freelance writers will have opportunities to write on a wide range of topics, perhaps across several websites. Writers who understand the Internet, wire communication devices, or multimedia software will have an advantage when searching for work. Some publishing companies can no longer afford to employ many full-time writers, and they

As more people turn to the Internet for their main source of information, industries and companies will need more skilled technical writers to write that information.

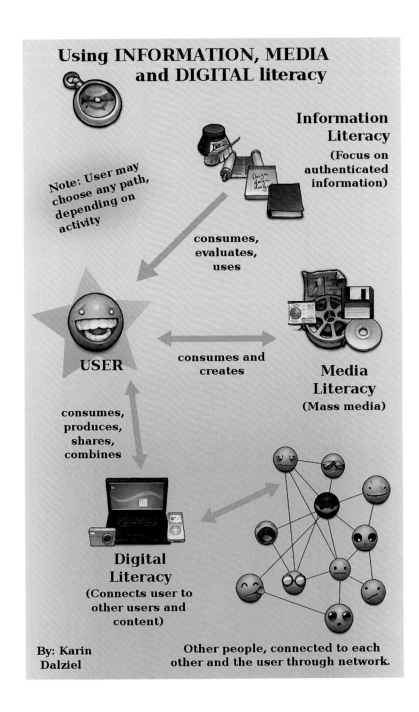

are predicted to continue having financial difficulty over the next few years. This means that, increasingly, these companies are turning to freelance writers to write for magazines, books, and newspapers. These workers are paid less but can still produce quality writing, making them a better investment for many publishers looking to cut back. In addition, nonprofit organizations will hire freelance writers in order to communicate messages to the public, either via the Web, print mailings, or newsletters.

JOB PROSPECTS

In the next few years, the number of writers looking for work will increase more than the number of jobs will. Writers looking for work will face more competition than they may have in the past. Writers starting out may have a hard time getting their first job because they are competing with workers with more experience. There will be a growing demand for written material overall, however, leading to more work for more people, particularly online. Many writers will find work for online publications or websites for existing publications. Businesses and organizations will also move their media, communications, and information online, necessitating quality writing, in many cases from freelancers. As it becomes less and less costly for individuals to publish their work, either online or in a variety of digital formats, more writers

There are many types of media used for information delivery in the modern world. As the methods of communication change, technical writers will need to evolve as well.

will have the opportunity to be published. In general, writers who understand the changing methods of communication will be the most competitive in the freelance writing job market.

TECHNICAL WRITERS: JOB OUTLOOK

As the technologies we use every day becomes more complicated, the demand for technical writers to explain these technologies grows. Employment of technical writers is projected to grow at 18 percent from 2008–2018. This rate of growth is faster than the average for all occupations. Competition for technical writing positions is expected to be moderate, with the number of people searching for technical writing jobs and the number of positions available about even.

EMPLOYMENT CHANGE

The high growth rate for techni-cal writing employment is due to advances in technology, the wide-spread use of the Internet, and the need for technical or scientific information on these topics. Busi-nesses need technical writers to explain

Did You Know?
8,900 technical writing jobs are expected to be added between 2008 and 2018.

more complicated communication *platforms* and assist customer service centers in moving to web-based communication, for example. As consumer electronic devices become more common, technical writers will be needed to write instruction manuals and user guides for this equipment.

As use of the Internet and other interactive media becomes more widespread, technical writers looking for work will be able to find many job opportunities working on the Web. Technical writers will be needed to produce technical content in a variety of web-based and interactive formats. The growing amount of information that companies and organizations choose to make available online requires that that content be of high quality. Professional technical writers are needed to make sure that information provided by companies and organizations over the Internet is technically accurate, useful to consumers, and easy to understand. As the Internet increasingly becomes a part of everyday life for businesses and individuals, demand for technical writers will grow.

Technical consulting firms and other professional services companies will continue to hire many technical writers. Though many more industries will require technical writing over the next decade, these companies will still be a good source of work for technical writers.

The ability to understand complex technical or scientific information and communicate that information so that it can be easily understood is a skill that will be in high demand over the next decade. Those hoping to become employed as technical writers can also benefit from knowledge in a specialized technical topic.

The following industries employ the most technical writers:

Industry	Employment	Hourly mean wage	Annual mean wage
Computer Systems Design and Related Services	8,860	$31.99	$66,540
Architectural, Engineering, and Related Services	3,470	$30.38	$63,190
Management, Scientific, and Technical Consulting Services	3,010	$31.09	$64,670
Software Publishers	2,880	$34.42	$71,590
Employment Services	2,310	$31.02	$64,510

(From http://www.bls.gov/oes/current/oes273042.htm)

JOB PROSPECTS

As the technology that people use every day becomes more and more complex, technical writers will be needed to explain those technologies to a growing number of users. This will result in increasing numbers of job opportunities for technical writers. The U.S. Department of Labor, Bureau of Labor Statistics projects that job prospects for those looking for work as technical writers will be good.

Over the next decade, experienced technical writers who have knowledge of a technical subject and good communication skills are likely to have the most job opportunities. Technical writers just starting their careers in the field will have a harder time finding desirable jobs than those with experience. Many technical writing positions will open, however, as experienced workers retire or move to other careers. Some technical writers who are freelancers may not make enough money to continue to work in the field and will need to leave the occupation—and this will create openings for those new to technical writing or other technical writers looking for work.

If You Have an Enterprising Personality . . .

You might be interested in one day starting your own publishing company or magazine—or working at the management level in an already existing company. This is the sort of career that can usually only be launched after several years of experience in the field. In the meantime, if you get a job in one of these companies to get you the experience you'll need, you can expect to earn an average salary of $51,980. Each year, there are about 8,790 of these positions.

If You Have a Conventional Personality . . .

Here are some of the best jobs for you as a writer.

JOB	ANNUAL EARNINGS	ANNUAL OPENINGS
technical writer	$64,210	47,460
translator	$43,130	36,610

FURTHER READING

Bly, Robert W. *Getting Started as a Freelance Writer.* Boulder, Col.: Sentient Publications, 2008.

Camenson, Blythe. *Careers in Writing.* New York: McGraw-Hill, 2007.

DeGalan, Julie and Stephen Lambert. *Great Jobs for English Majors.* New York: McGraw Hill, 2006.

Glatzer, Jenna. *Make a Real Living as a Freelance Writer.* White River Junction, Ver.: Nomad Press, 2004.

Gould, Jay. *Opportunities in Technical Writing Careers.* New York: McGraw-Hill, 2008.

FIND OUT MORE ON THE INTERNET

The American Society of Journalists and Authors
www.asja.org

Career Compass
www.careervoyages.gov/careercompass-main.cfm

Freelance Writing Jobs: A Freelance Writing Community and Freelance Writing Jobs Resource
www.freelancewritinggigs.com

Self-Employment Resources and Services: United States Government
www.usa.gov/Business/Self_Employed.shtml

Society for Technical Communication
www.stc.org

DISCLAIMER

The websites listed on this page were active at the time of publication. The publisher is not responsible for websites that have changed their address or discontinued operation since the date of publication. The publisher will review and update the websites upon each reprint.

BIBLIOGRAPHY

Business Week. "A Guide to Self Employment," www.businessweek.com/smallbiz/content/jan2009/sb20090123_156963.htm (3 March 2010).

United States Department of Labor, Bureau of Labor Statistics. "Authors, Writers, and Editors," www.bls.gov/oco/ocos320.htm (2 March 2010).

United States Department of Labor, Bureau of Labor Statistics. "Interpreters and Translators," www.bls.gov/oco/ocos175.htm (2 March 2010).

United States Department of Labor, Bureau of Labor Statisics. "News Analysts, Reporters, and Correspondents," www.bls.gov/oco/ocos088.htm (2 March 2010).

United States Department of Labor, Bureau of Labor Statisics. "Technical Writers," www.bls.gov/oco/ocos319.htm (2 March 2010).

United States Department of Labor, Bureau of Labor Statistics. "You're A What? Greeting Card Writer," www.bls.gov/opub/ooq/2001/Fall/yawhat.pdf (2 March 2010).

INDEX

PICTURE CREDITS

Creative Commons Attribution 2.0 Generic/Unported
    blmurch: pg. 53
    Bright Meadow: pg. 41
    dbdbrobot: pg. 19
    Ed Yourdon: pg. 26
    MechanicJosh: pg. 13
    moriza: pg. 38
    quaziefoto: pg. 50

Dreamstime.com
    Sergey Kravtsov: pg. 8

United States Air Force
    Laura Max: pg. 33

To the best knowledge of the publisher, all images not specifically credited are in the public domain. If any image has been inadvertently uncredited, please notify Harding House Publishing Service, 220 Front Street, Vestal, New York 13850, so that credit can be given in future printings.

About the Author

Camden Flath is a writer living and working in Binghamton, New York. He has a degree in English and has written several books for young people. He is interested in current political, social, and economic issues and applies those interests to his writing.

About the Consultant

Michael Puglisi is the director of the Department of Labor's Workforce New York One Stop Center in Binghamton, New York. He has also held several leadership positions in the International Association of Workforce Professionals (IAWP), a non-profit educational association exclusively dedicated to workforce professionals with a rich tradition and history of contributions to workforce excellence. IAWP members receive the tools and resources they need to effectively contribute to the workforce development system daily. By providing relevant education, timely and informative communication and valuable findings of pertinent research, IAWP equips its members with knowledge, information and practical tools for success. Through its network of local and regional chapters, IAWP is preparing its members for the challenges of tomorrow.